ENG
&CHANG

The Original
Siamese Twins

ENG & CHANG

The Original Siamese Twins

DAVID R. COLLINS

A People in Focus Book

 **DILLON PRESS**
New York

Maxwell Macmillan Canada
Toronto
Maxwell Macmillan International
New York   Oxford   Singapore   Sydney

Photo Credits

Photo research by Debbie Needleman

Cover courtesy of the Boston Public Library, Print Department, Americana Collection
Back cover courtesy of the Harvard Theatre Collection

Harvard Theatre Collection: 8, 29, 49, 57, 59, 62, 69, 105, 108, 113, 121; Peabody and Essex Museum: 42-43, 114; Boston Public Library: 45, 56; Southern Historical Collection, University of North Carolina at Chapel Hill: 66, 86, 92, 118; The Barnum Museum: 94, 96; James Callahan: 122.

Book design by Carol Matsuyama

Library of Congress Cataloging-in-Publication Data

Collins, David R.
    Eng and Chang : the original Siamese twins / by David R. Collins. —
1st ed.
      p. cm. — (People in focus)
    Includes bibliographical references and index.
    Summary: A biography of Eng and Chang, the congenitally united twins born in Siam (Thailand) in 1811.
    ISBN 0-87518-602-5 HC   ISBN 0-382-24719-1 PBK
    1. Bunker, Chang, 1811–1874—Juvenile literature. 2. Bunker, Eng, 1811–1874—Juvenile literature. 3. Siamese twins—United States—Biography—Juvenile literature. 4. Siamese twins—North Carolina—Biography—Juvenile literature. [1. Bunker, Chang, 1811–1874. 2. Bunker, Eng, 1811–1874. 3. Siamese twins.] I. Title. II. Series.
QM691.B86C65   1994
362.4—dc20
[B]   93-26295

Dillon Press
Macmillan Publishing Company
866 Third Avenue
New York, NY 10022

Maxwell Macmillan Canada, Inc.
1200 Eglinton Avenue East
Suite 200
Don Mills, Ontario M3C 3N1

Macmillan Publishing Company is part of the Maxwell Communication Group of Companies.

First edition

Printed in the United States of America

10 9 8 7 6 5 4 3 2 1

Contents

Throughout history, there have been people like Eng and Chang Bunker who have risen above handicaps and obstacles. In reading their stories, others may find the strength and courage to overcome their own troubles. This book is respectfully dedicated to the human spirit that these two men possessed, as well as to our own human spirit, which could help create a better world.

/ Introduction

Do you have a little brother or sister who is always following you around? Maybe it is a friend who seems to be with you all the time—whether it's your choice or not. It seems impossible to ever do anything alone or have any privacy.

In the pages that follow, you will share in one of the most unusual stories ever recorded in history. Eng and Chang Bunker were born almost two centuries ago in the country of Siam, which is now called Thailand. At their birth the two baby boys were sentenced to die by order of Siam's king. Why? The two infants were joined together at the chest, and the king thought this was an evil sign. Death seemed an appropriate punishment.

Thankfully, the sentence was not carried out. Although physically attached, Eng and Chang Bunker lived lives full of fascinating experiences. As you read their story, you will share those experiences. After you have finished the book, you will probably never again complain about your little brother or sister or friend following you around.

Chapter / One

Dark Shadows

Something was wrong.

Something was seriously wrong.

"Can't you move, Chang?" Eng Bunker stared at his brother. "Let's go to our cabin."

Chang Bunker did not answer. He sat motionless, looking down at the chessboard in front of him.

Eng started to stand up. But it was useless. If Chang did not move, Eng could not. The bond that joined the two men was no usual feeling of love between two brothers. It was a physical attachment. Chang and Eng Bunker were Siamese twins, joined together since birth by a thick band of flesh at the lower chest. It was like an arm between the two. Where one brother went,

Eng and Chang, the original Siamese twins

the other had to go. When one brother stood up, so did the other. If one brother wanted to go to bed, the other brother had to go, too. Together. All their lives they had done everything together.

But now, on this August day in the year 1870, something was wrong, terribly wrong. As a trans-atlantic steamer sailed toward New York City, the two Bunker brothers were helped to their cabin inside the ship. It was clear that Chang Bunker had suffered a stroke, a stroke that left him unable to move his right arm, side, and leg. His brother Eng Bunker felt fine, yet he had no choice but to also stay in the cabin below. Hopefully, the paralysis would pass. Perhaps being back in the United States would help Chang's recovery.

But when the steamship docked in New York Harbor, concern increased over the health of the famous Bunker brothers. Chang showed no improvement. Doctors were called in and examinations made. Yet little action was taken. The case was so strange, so complicated. Trained people in medicine hesitated to take action for fear of making a mistake.

Sadly the two brothers returned to their homes in Mount Airy, North Carolina. Their wives and their children welcomed them home. In both cases it was a big welcoming party. Nine of Chang's children, ranging in age from nearly 2 to 25, still lived at home. For Eng, it was six children, aged 5 to 25, who resided at home. Both of the Bunker farms relied on the help of family workers.

Slowly Chang began to regain his strength. Little by little, movement returned to his entire body. He would never be as he was before, but doctors told Chang he was lucky to be as healthy as he was.

In the years that followed, Chang and Eng Bunker slowed their pace. There was no more helping to feed the cattle, pigs, and sheep. There was no more helping to plant the wheat and oats. The twins simply climbed in a buggy and allowed one of their children to drive them around their farms, which sat side by side. They waved to those working, wishing they could help, too. But those days were gone.

In April 1873, 11-year-old Lizzie, Chang's daughter, offered to take her father and uncle for a buggy ride. Soon after starting, the horse suddenly lurched. A frightened Lizzie leaped out of the buggy, breaking her hand as she fell. The carriage careened ahead, the two helpless men unable to grab the reins. Reaching a turn in the road, the horse swung the buggy over. Eng and Chang fell out. Both of them were battered and bruised.

After the accident little news about Eng and

Chang Bunker drifted out of Mount Airy. Now and then word circulated that the brothers had died and been quietly laid to rest. A writer for the *Wilmington Morning Star* reported that, during the summer of 1873, Eng and Chang were indulging "freely in intoxicating beverages." There were also rumors that the Bunker brothers had tired of public attention and wanted privacy. Many people found the latter story quite believable. For decades the original Siamese twins had been watched, inspected, and studied. All over the world they had visited doctors, and doctors had traveled to Mount Airy, too. Now, perhaps Eng and Chang wanted to spend their final years quietly.

As 1874 began, both Chang and Eng appeared quite healthy. On January 12 they entertained a guest in Chang's home. He later told others that the brothers "received me very courteously indeed."

But during the night of January 12, everything changed. Chang began coughing, and he complained of chest pains. Dr. Joseph Hollingsworth, the family physician, was sent for. Since he was out of town, his brother, Dr. William Hollingsworth, hurried to the farmhouse of Chang Bunker. Bronchitis was diagnosed, and Chang was ordered to stay in bed. Naturally, Eng was forced to do the same.

Chang felt better during the next few days. By

January 15 he seemed much stronger. He insisted on making plans to go to Eng's home a mile away. That was their usual schedule—three days in one brother's house, and three days in the other brother's house. At the end of the third day, they traveled to the other's house to begin the next three days there.

Adelaide Bunker, Chang's wife, argued with her husband. She wanted him to stay at home. The air was freezing outside. Why risk future illness? Eng agreed to stay at his brother's home.

But no, Chang would not hear of such a thing. He felt strong enough, and a deal was a deal. It was time to go to Eng's home, and that is where they would go. The matter was settled. The two brothers bundled up, climbed into their open carriage, and headed down the rough and icy road to Eng's home. The bitter winter air bit into their faces as the buggy rolled along. Eng snapped the reins hard, eager to reach his destination.

Sallie, Eng's wife, was waiting with a hot meal on the stove and a blazing fire in the fireplace. But Chang could not stop shaking. He shook while eating, his legs and feet wrapped in quilts and blankets. Eng wanted to do some things around the house now that he was home, but Chang resisted. All he wanted to do was go to bed. Again, Eng gave in to his brother's wishes.

It was a sleepless night for Chang. Chest pains returned. At times, he actually felt as if he were dying. Surprisingly, Eng felt fine the next morning, having enjoyed a good night's rest. He was eager to set about his tasks, but Chang kept complaining while his brother worked. When nighttime arrived, he had no desire to go to bed. In fact, he said, "It would kill me to lie down." Eng sat in front of the fire, hoping and praying his brother would tire.

Meanwhile, among the scattered farmhouses on the North Carolina countryside, word spread that "the Bunker brothers were ailin'." William Hollingsworth was better at doctoring than keeping secrets. People around Mount Airy considered Eng and Chang more like family than neighbors. The story of their lives had been told and retold as each child in the area reached an age to understand just what had happened.

"It all started a long time ago," one of the older folks would begin, "in a country called Siam . . ."

Chapter / Two

Face-to-Face

The date was May 11, 1811.

The place was Siam, a country in Southeast Asia that would someday be known as Thailand. In one of the many river inlets near the village of Meklong, a houseboat rocked lazily in the water. But inside the vessel there was much activity.

A Chinese fisherman, Ti-eye, tried to keep his wife comfortable as she prepared to give birth. At 35, the woman named Nok had already brought four children into the world. The couple hoped to have many more. Couples with many sons and daughters enjoyed much respect in Siam.

As was the custom in Siam, a midwife was there to

help Nok have her baby. The pregnant woman showed little fear. As the final moments for delivery arrived, Ti-eye left the room. By late afternoon, word of the events that had taken place in the houseboat spread quickly among the villagers. Nok had given birth to twins, both boys. The rest of the news traveled in hushed whispers. The twins were joined at the breastbone by a mysterious extra arm, a thick ligament of flesh. The two babies were one and could not be separated.

To the father, Ti-eye, the joined brothers were still his sons, worthy of names and love. The infant on the twins' own right appeared quieter, more peaceful. He was called Eng, which in Siamese means "strictly, to tie strongly." The other child seemed to be more irritable and demanding. He was named Chang, which means "unsavory" or "tasteless."

When news of the strange and unusual birth reached the king of Siam, he decided the babies should be put to death. King Rama II thought such a birth was an evil sign, an omen that something bad was going to happen. Maybe the world was going to end. The ruler ordered the infants put to death.

At the same time, doctors in the kingdom were suggesting ways to separate the two babies. One proposed using a red-hot wire to cut the two infants apart. Another thought a saw could be used. Someone said that if the two babies were hung across a fine catgut cord, they would gradually separate; since the ligament would rip apart slowly, it would heal as it divided. Strange ideas? Perhaps. But doctors back in 1811 had little knowledge and training with these Siamese twins.

Medical records did exist for over 100 sets of twins born attached in some way, although none of the infants were joined at the chest. Many had died in operations to separate them. Others survived their childhood years but died early into adulthood.

All the commotion about her twins did not take Nok away from her duties as a mother. She paid no attention to the talk that her two babies were under a sentence of death. Nor would she listen to the suggestions of doctors as to how Chang and Eng might be separated. Every idea sounded painful and uncertain. The mother wanted nothing to do with anything that would endanger the lives of her two sons. Quietly she went about the tasks that needed to be done. Nok bathed her infants, fed and loved them. When no disaster occurred, King Rama II withdrew his decree of death for the two boys. Learning that Nok and Ti-eye wanted no help in separating Chang and Eng, the doctors stopped talking about it. Life returned to normal under the thatched roof of the fisherman's houseboat.

Truthfully, though, things could never be normal again. Visitors often appeared at Ti-eye's home. They did not come to buy the fish he sold from the doorway. No, they came to see for themselves the babies sleeping face-to-face. Of the 10,000 people in the Meklong village, there was not a soul who did not know about Chang and Eng. Strangers kept a close eye on the houseboat, eager to catch a peek at the two joined babies.

Ti-eye and Nok tired of the constant attention. They wanted to give Chang and Eng, as well as their other four children, a normal childhood. They had enough problems without those brought by strangers.

Weeks slipped into months. Learning to walk proved a big obstacle to Chang and Eng. Crawling was easy, but standing up was a challenge. Walking forward seemed impossible. But slowly, ever so slowly, the two young boys sensed how they had to use their bodies together in order to move forward. They had to understand gravity first of all, how to stand up in one place. Then they had to take turns stepping ahead. It took practice, repeating the same movements again and again.

As Chang and Eng walked along the Meklong

River one morning, they heard music coming from a riverboat. They wanted to get closer, and suddenly they tumbled into the water. They splashed and thrashed around wildly. They struggled to regain their balance, but they could not. The boys drifted away from shore, yelling and flailing about. The crew of a nearby boat rescued them.

Once they were able to walk, the twins also began running. The people of Meklong village stood amazed as they watched the two joined brothers race down the streets. Often Chang and Eng darted to the top of a hill, wrapped their arms securely around each other, and rolled down. They laughed all the way.

Everything was fine as long as the two brothers timed their movements perfectly. But a split second's difference could bring painful results.

Once the boys sprinted across a field. In their path sat a low fence. Together they lifted their legs to cover the jump. But their timing was off just a bit. One twin made it; the other did not. They dangled, one on each side of the fence. Their screams revealed their agonizing pain. Finally one of them lifted himself over the fence to join the other. The fleshy ligament was badly bruised, and the boys had to rest for days.

Ti-eye and Nok had no intention of spoiling their two joined sons. Eng and Chang were expected to do what the other children did. In fact, the boys sometimes bragged that they could do tasks twice as easily as anyone else. After all, there were two of them! Soon they were helping their father fish. Ti-eye kept a small craft tied to the raft that formed the floor of the houseboat, which was permanently secured to the bank of the Meklong River. Both boys learned how to use oars and paddled the boat swiftly through the water. Sometimes they jumped out of their boat and swam in tandem. Their arms and legs grew stronger each year.

With all the work and exercise, the ligament stretched. From a face-to-face position as infants, Eng and Chang began to stand and move side by side. Usually one twin's arm was tossed over the other twin's shoulder. The flesh bond between them lengthened to 5 1/2 inches. But still Ti-eye and Nok made no effort to have the ligament cut apart. The loving parents feared that such an operation might kill one or both of their children.

Diseases, too, posed a constant problem. When one brother caught a cold, the other soon followed. There was no way, of course, of keeping the brothers apart when one got sick. Smallpox, that dreaded mixture of fever and virus, hit both twins when they were six years old. For weeks they lay in their room in the bamboo houseboat. Fortunately, the illness did not leave the scars it so often left behind.

But fights against disease were only one kind of battle Chang and Eng waged. Sometimes they fought against each other. Chang was of a more sour nature, seldom smiling and often finding fault with his brother. Eng was easier to please. If there was an argument, it was Eng who usually gave in and let Chang have his own way.

There came a time, however, when Eng would *not* give in. Chang wanted to go outside, and Eng did not. The boys shouted at each other, then began pounding as hard as they could. Their screams brought their mother running, but not before the brothers had bloodied noses and red skin from slaps and hits.

Angry and frustrated, Nok sat Chang and Eng down for a serious talk. They *had* to get along. Never could they fight like other people. Others could have disagreements and stay away from each other. Chang and Eng could not.

Shortly after their bout with smallpox, Chang and Eng began to receive lessons. Their teacher spent extra time with the two boys, making sure they could both write legibly. Eng proved patient and careful, while Chang hurried to get finished. Again their mother sat the boys down and tried to impress upon them the importance of trying to do the best they could.

In 1819 disaster struck Southeast Asia. It was not in the form of deadly typhoons and torrential monsoon rains. The people of Siam and its neighboring countries were used to those visitors. But no one knew how to deal with the vicious disease called cholera. It swept across the countryside, visiting single families living in rural areas as well as families living in villages and cities. Doctors stood helplessly by, unable to offer precaution, treatment, or remedy.

Meklong was not spared. In each home along the river town, men and women, boys and girls, fell victim to cholera. The disease hit swiftly, weakening each victim through constant vomiting and diarrhea. Often in a matter of hours, the patient was dead.

Everywhere there were bodies. Families were frequently too sick to bury their dead. "Take the bodies to the river" came the order from the authorities. To the shores of the Meklong the bodies were carried, then tossed into the water. Tragically, there was not always enough current to carry the victims away. Bodies rotted, and flies feasted, carrying germs to new, unsuspecting people in the village.

Ti-eye and Nok were trapped in their home with their children. By this time there were nine youngsters, including Chang and Eng. They dared not go out, for in every other nearby house there was danger and death. There were no customers for fish. Food supplies grew scarce. Then, one by one, the children began getting sick. There was no way of holding off the dreaded cholera.

One, two, three—each passing day brought the death of another of Ti-eye and Nok's children. Two more died during the second week of the epidemic. How painful it must have been for the tired fisherman to carry the lifeless bodies of his sons and daughters to the river's edge and slip them into the water. Somehow Chang and Eng managed to stay strong.

And then it was Ti-eye himself who came down with cholera. A frightened and tired Nok brought the sick man food and cared for him. It was too much, too great a struggle for the fisherman. In a week the man was dead.

The Buddhist religion called for special services whenever the head of a household died. Eight-year-old Chang and Eng never forgot the events of their father's funeral. Both of them wrote and spoke later about the services.

Nok led her remaining four children to the courtyard of the Buddhist temple in Meklong. Ti-eye's coffin, covered with a red-and-gold cloth, rested on a platform six feet above the ground. A canopy of white cloth, the color of mourning, draped the area. Long chains of colorful flowers hung on all sides of the canopy.

The sound of a Siamese flute broke the silence. Then another joined in, followed by the soft sounds of drums and gongs. Chang and Eng were glad there was music. Their father had loved music, and they did, too.

A Buddhist priest appeared nearby and began reading a prayer. A small circle of women lit candles, humming as they moved silently at their holy task. Then the priest moved toward the coffin. Other priests appeared, and carefully they removed a strip of cloth from the coffin. The cloth was cut, and a piece was given to Nok. Each of the children received a piece, too.

Slowly the priests lifted the coffin and carried it inside the temple. Chang and Eng watched, wondering where their father's body was being taken. Their older brother Noy answered their silent question. He told them their father's body was being washed and purified in the temple.

Dried brush and twigs were placed on the platform where the coffin had rested. When the priests returned, they placed the body gently on the platform. Then they gave out candles to those attending. Once the candles were lit, those holding them moved forward and lit the brush and twigs. Soon flames leaped skyward.

After the body was cremated, only one final act remained in the Buddhist service. Nok took coins from a pouch she carried. She wandered over to a group of beggars from the village and gave them out. Then she returned to her children and led them home.

Chang and Eng carried good memories of their father. Ti-eye had been a kind and loving parent, a hardworking fisherman, a man of pride and honor. But he was not a rich man. There were no funds left to support a widow and four children. The small houseboat on the Meklong River was no longer filled with the sounds of children laughing. The future looked grim for this family. In a few short weeks disease had stolen the head of the household and five of his children. Chang and Eng were frightened, afraid that something might take away the rest of their family. For the first time in a long while, the two eight-year-old boys did not mind being joined together. Somehow it gave them a sense of security. More than once during these sad times, the twin brothers cried themselves to sleep in each other's arms.

Chapter / Three

Off to See the King

Ti-eye had been a good fisherman. His children had
never gone hungry. Now Nok became the provider.
Since there were plenty of coconuts in the area, she
decided to grind them down and make oil from them.
It was slow and difficult work. Soon she looked for
another way to make money.

Nok decided to sell notions, such as pins, needles,
and thread. Dealers sailed along the Meklong. Nok
bought small shipments, then sold the notions to the
villagers. She used the same table her husband had
used to sell his fish. But the business brought in little
money.

To help their family, Eng and Chang offered to

work. Nok told her two sons that they were too young. Anyway, what could they do?

Eng and Chang decided to show their mother they could make money. Often they had fished with their father. The two boys knew many of the other fishermen. One agreed to let them help him.

Early in the morning the two boys would set off. Hour after hour Eng and Chang worked, pulling in loads of fish. By the time they returned, the brothers were tired. But they were proud of what they had done.

Days slipped into weeks. Carefully the twins saved the money they earned. In two years they were ready to go into business for themselves. They bought their own boat.

Fishing was not easy work for two ten-year-old boys. Soon they found a means to make more money than fishing provided. They rowed to many huts along the Meklong River. At each one they bought different wares—notions, food, and items of clothing. Then they sold them for more money at the river marketplace. Customers were fascinated by the mysterious arm that bound the two together. It helped the boys make more sales. Even the Siamese government helped them, charging smaller taxes because of the twins' handicap.

One year drifted into another. By the time Eng and

Chang were teenagers, they considered themselves successful Meklong merchants. People spoke of their good business sense. They knew how to buy the cheapest goods, then resell them for the greatest profit. Nok kept the money her sons earned, paying the family bills and saving some, too.

Often Eng and Chang stayed all night on their boat. That way they could get an early start in the morning. But one day, as the sun came up, the local police arrested Eng and Chang. Other river peddlers were arrested, too. All were brought in for questioning. Someone had stolen another merchant's supply of peacock feathers.

No one would admit to the crime. Chang and Eng said they knew nothing about the feathers. The chief of police ordered all those questioned to drink a strange liquid. He was convinced the thief would vomit. It was a weird system of justice, but no one dared argue with the chief of police. Eng and Chang each drank, their faces worried and pale. Neither of the twins vomited. One of the other peddlers *did* throw up. He was beaten and thrown in jail. Later that day the real thief was found. He still had the peacock feathers in his boat.

Fishermen and their families looked forward to seeing the two brothers on the river. When Chang

By the time Eng and Chang were teenagers, they were successful river merchants.

and Eng stopped to sell their goods, they always told people when they would return. That way there was a crowd waiting when they came back. They knew how to do business.

In 1825, shortly after becoming king of Siam, Rama III heard about the joined brothers of Meklong. People called Eng and Chang the Chinese Twins because their parents were from China. King Rama III wanted to meet them. He invited the 14-year-old boys to visit him at the palace in Bangkok, 60 miles away.

Nok could not believe the news! Her two sons were going to the royal court. She was invited, too, along with her other children. But it was clear that the king really wanted to see Eng and Chang. Nok worried that the boys would not appear well dressed. She found the best suits she could, then sewed the jackets carefully so the ligament barely showed.

Off they sailed—Nok, Chang, Eng, and their surviving sister. Their craft was a good-sized junk that slipped smoothly through the water. The twins took along a supply of preserved duck eggs. Duck eggs were a special treat in Southeast Asia. The twins hoped to trade the eggs in Bangkok. Then they would buy supplies to bring back to Meklong.

The Meklong River was dotted by small fishing boats and other junks. As Eng and Chang drifted closer to Bangkok, they saw the tall Buddhist temples rising toward the sky. Floating peddlers called out, wanting to sell their fish and fresh pork.

Suddenly a giant craft with bright-colored banners approached their boat. King Rama had sent special representatives to meet and greet his guests. The king's men gave the boys presents of fruit and tea. The food was welcome after the 60-mile voyage. "You are to come with us," Eng and Chang were told. The twins were whisked away by carriage to a private house. No one in Bangkok was going to see the unusual visitors before King Rama III met them the next morning.

Eng and Chang were excited about getting to see Siam's royal leader. But their mother, Nok, was even more excited. Over and over she prepared her sons for their important meeting. She tidied up their handsome suits. She gave them instructions on how to bow. It was easier for other guests who were not joined. Eng and Chang practiced and practiced.

At 8:30 the next morning, the king's special representative appeared. He took the twins to the royal barge. Oarsmen in bright red uniforms rowed them to the outer gate of the palace. There two strong men waited to lift them in a giant hammock. The muscular duo carried Chang and Eng across the courtyard and through another gate. Once inside, they moved along a row of sheds. The king's finest cannon rested inside. Chang and Eng looked farther down the avenue. Mammoth elephants moved to their trainers' orders. The ground shook under their feet. Finally, at a third gate, the twins reached their destination.

The hammock was lowered. Carefully Chang and Eng climbed out. They looked around and saw the Royal Palace, the giant Buddhist temple, and the

Audience Hall. Chang and Eng followed their host to
the Audience Hall. It was a tall, long, red room with
gold trim along the sides and ceiling. It was the
grandest room Eng and Chang had ever seen.

The twins took off their shoes. People did not
appear before the king of Siam with their shoes on.
Rama III sat on his throne, which was raised 15 feet
from the floor, in the middle of the room. Slowly the
two boys moved forward. Then they stopped, dropped
to their knees, and touched their foreheads to the
ground. Once more they stood up and inched forward.
Again they fell to the floor, bowed their heads against
the ground. Nine times they repeated the action.
Finally, when they were close enough, they spoke to
the king. "Exalted Lord, Sovereign of many Princes, let
the Lord of Lives tread upon his slave's head."

As practiced, the two boys greeted the king. He, in
turn, asked them many questions. Minutes slipped
away as Eng and Chang shared the stories of their
lives back home, how they fished and lived together.
King Rama III was fascinated. Finally he nodded to a
guard. Giant gongs clashed and echoed through the
great room. The interview was over.

The minute the king left, others in the courtroom
surrounded Eng and Chang. Everyone wanted to talk
to the two brothers. People carefully inspected the

ligament, exclaiming how well the boys got along.

From the Audience Hall Eng and Chang were led to the Royal Palace, where they met all 35 of the king's wives. Again the questions flowed. The women marveled at all the brothers could do in spite of their handicap.

Next it was on to the king's royal stables. Never had Eng and Chang seen such grand ponies. The proud animals pranced and danced, their sleek coats glistening. Still there were more sights to see.

The twins followed the king's guide to a covered passageway. Paintings of the royal family dotted the walls. Into the Temple of Gautama the visitors walked. It was a plastered brick building, its wooden inner walls carved by hand. Statues of birds and serpents rested atop handsome pillars. The temple altar was covered with gold Buddhas, including the 2,000-year-old Emerald Buddha. Hundreds of gems within the image dazzled all who gazed upon it.

For the two 14-year-old boys, the trip was unbelievable! They were speechless as they left the temple. Meeting the king—the royal horses—the paintings—the Temple of Gautama—so much to remember to share with family and friends. To top it all off, King Rama III showered Eng and Chang with gifts to take back home.

What a homecoming the boys received! Neighbors

along the Meklong River lined the shores. Few of the fisherfolk had ever been to Bangkok, much less seen the king. Chang and Eng told stories by the hour, one twin filling in the details the other twin left out.

The two boys were eager to make use of their new supplies. Nok had sold the preserved eggs in Bangkok. Although the twins appreciated the gifts King Rama had supplied, they sold them to other Meklong merchants. Chang and Eng had plans for their money.

Soon the twins owned a duck preserve near the family houseboat. The animals waddled and quacked freely, enjoying their privacy. Chang and Eng brought back shellfish from the Gulf of Siam for their ducks to feast upon. Good food made for more eggs. The twins dipped each duck egg into soft clay and salt for preserving, then covered it with dry ashes. After the ashes were cleaned off, each egg stayed tasty and fresh for up to three years. Such eggs were considered a delicacy among the rich. Business prospered. The twins sold over 10,000 eggs a year. Chang and Eng were considered among the best merchants in Meklong—and they were only 15 years old.

Another respected merchant in Siam was a man named Robert Hunter. He had come from Scotland, and his family had made money manufacturing glass and linen. Hunter himself owned ships and exported goods from Siam to many parts of the world. A friend of the king, the Scottish businessman was always looking for a way to increase his fortune.

From the first time Hunter saw Eng and Chang, he was amazed. He was standing on a boat in the Meklong River when he noticed the twins swimming. They looked like a strange animal with two heads, four legs, and four arms. Hunter stopped to talk with the boys and enjoyed them completely. Nok invited Hunter to dinner, and he became a family friend.

"They have no pity for themselves," the Scottish businessman wrote in 1826. "They move and act as one being. Unless a person can view the spectacle for himself, it is impossible to describe."

Clearly, Robert Hunter was thinking along those lines—of letting others view the twins as he had done. Although he enjoyed being a friend to the boys, he was always thinking as a businessman. Surely Eng and Chang would be a fine export—to America, Great Britain, and who knew where else?

But before Hunter could pursue his idea, King Rama III jumped in. He was sending a delegation to Cochin China—a country that today is part of southern Vietnam—and decided that Chang and Eng should go along. The king wanted to make new trade agreements with the Cochin Chinese government. The twins had impressed the king during their visit to Bangkok. Perhaps they would also impress the emperor of Cochin China. It might help in the business dealings between the two countries.

Off the twins sailed in the fall of 1827, traveling first south in the Gulf of Siam and then north in the South China Sea. They were heading for the emperor's palace in Hue. They stopped at numerous ports along the coast. At each place, Chang and Eng noticed the shops and displays of the merchants. They were eager to bring new ideas back home.

The people of Cochin China cheerfully welcomed the Siamese visitors. While the business officials met, Chang and Eng were allowed the freedom to travel. Sometimes they rode on top of elephants.

The sprawling bazaar in Saigon (present-day Ho Chi Minh City) attracted the twins. They roamed throughout the shops, handling the fine silks and carved figurines. The grand porcelain statues caught their attention, too. For hours the two boys spoke with the merchants, picking up business tips.

Then it was on to a giant arena where elephants fought tigers. The Cochin Chinese had little use for tigers and had declawed the creatures and sewed their mouths shut. Chang and Eng watched as the huge tusked beasts destroyed countless cats. It was not a pleasant sight. The twins loved animals. They silently watched the ugly spectacle, not wanting to offend their hosts. Yet the slaughter troubled them, and they suffered horrible nightmares from what they witnessed. They were glad to leave the area.

From Saigon the twins sailed slowly up the coast. They grew eager to complete their mission for King Rama III and meet the emperor of Cochin China. Finally they reached Hue, and the day of the audience approached.

Once more Chang and Eng practiced the speeches they would make before a ruler. When that moment came, Chang and Eng were ready. They spoke freely, answering any and all questions. They were surprised to learn from the emperor that there were supposedly a number of joined twins in his own land. They had no way of knowing that he was lying. The proud ruler would never admit that tiny Siam could produce something Cochin China could not. Once again Chang and Eng left carrying many fine gifts.

King Rama III was delighted with the twins' performance. They had represented Siam well. The Siamese ruler showered more gifts on his two young ambassadors of goodwill. As before, they sold the gifts and invested the money in their duck farm.

Not long after the twins returned to Meklong,

Robert Hunter came to visit them. It was clear to him that the brothers enjoyed traveling and meeting new people. Hunter told them stories about great countries across the sea. There were sights too grand to be believed! Chang and Eng listened attentively. So did Nok, their mother. Although she loved her two sons dearly, she would not stand in their way if they decided to go abroad. Yet she wanted to make sure they would be treated properly.

But would King Rama III be willing to let Eng and Chang go? The Siamese ruler was fond of the twins and might be planning to use them again for government dealings. Hunter spoke to another friend, Abel Coffin, a trader and ship's captain. Coffin had done business with the king, and Hunter enlisted Coffin's help. They agreed to become partners managing Eng and Chang.

Hunter and Coffin convinced King Rama III that he should let the twins go. The ruler appreciated the work that the businessmen had done in his country. He was also satisfied that Chang and Eng would be well treated.

Nok proved harder to convince. After all, Hunter's plans called for her sons to be gone for over two years. Would they be handled with respect? She did not want them to be displayed publicly as freaks. And what about money? Chang and Eng were her chief means of support.

Hunter and Coffin promised that the twins would appear in America and Great Britain as honored guests. They would be treated with respect and dignity. Captain Coffin agreed to send money back to Nok if profits were made through the boys' appearances.

On March 31, 1829, Chang and Eng bid Meklong farewell. It was not easy for the 17-year-old boys to say good-bye to family and friends. But they would be back.

Or would they?

Chapter/Four

Ahoy, America!

Chang and Eng stood in the crow's nest on the main mast of the American ship *Sachem*. The boys scanned the sea around them, looking for any sight of land. The ship's sails billowed in the afternoon breezes. Captain Abel Coffin roamed the two decks of the vessel below, making sure all was well.

The Siamese twins became instant favorites of the *Sachem* crew. The boys enjoyed climbing the masts and helping the cook prepare meals. They listened to the orders called out and often called them out, too. Each day they learned new words and phrases in English by listening and repeating. Someday, they hoped, they would captain their own ship.

Weeks slipped into months as the *Sachem* cut through the waters of the Indian Ocean and then out into the Atlantic. Less hearty souls took sick, but Chang and Eng proved able travelers. Overeating rich Western food sent them to their bed for a day, and a toothache was a three-day agony. But for the most part, the twins enjoyed the cruise.

On August 16, 1829, the *Sachem* slipped gracefully into Boston Harbor. The journey took 138 days. Chang and Eng left the ship with countless memories of helping the ship's crew.

As the boys descended the gangplank, a reporter for the *Boston Patriot* was waiting. Captain Coffin was not only a worthy seaman but a skilled promoter. He planned to turn the Siamese twins into a special attraction for the city's 61,000 residents.

But before showing Chang and Eng to Boston, Coffin arranged to show the city to the twins. By horse-drawn carriage the boys rode through the streets. They gazed and gawked at the stone and brick buildings, with glass windows—so different from the bamboo structures of Meklong. Handsome carriages clattered over cobblestone streets. Women in silks and satins exited their vehicles on the arms of gentlemen. It amazed the Siamese visitors that none of those men wore his hair braided down the back in a queue.

The Sachem, the ship that brought Eng and Chang to Boston in 1829

Chang and Eng provided doctors in Boston with a few surprises, too. Dr. John Collins Warren of the Harvard Medical School gave the twins a thorough examination. He found the hard substance joining the boys to be two inches long at its upper edge and about five inches long at the lower edge. It measured four inches downward and two inches horizontally, and could stretch to almost eight inches. Always the twins moved together, never pulling the cord separately. It was as if each anticipated the other's thoughts. The cord seemed to be made up of cartilage. Could the boys be cut apart?

Dr. Warren shied away from such an idea for two reasons. Medically, there could be continuous tissue within the attached ligament that would make surgery dangerous. More important, he did not feel that Eng and Chang were psychologically ready for such an operation. Until they were, or unless one were to die before the other at some time, Warren opposed any efforts to separate the twins.

Other famous doctors agreed with Dr. Warren. Their comments helped publicize the twins in the city. Hunter and Coffin hired a Boston native, James Webster Hale, to help promote the twins in America. Only ten years older than Chang and Eng, Hale became their lifelong friend.

Boston Courier.

VOL. V.---NO. 1698.   SATURDAY, AUGUST 22, 1829.   PRICE EIGHT DOLLARS.

GREAT NATURAL CURIOSITY.

JUST arrived from Siam in the ship Sachem, capt. Coffin, two Siamese youths who are connected together at the extremity of the breast bone by an elastic ligament about five inches in length and three in breadth; they will be exhibited at the Exchange Coffee House for a few days previous to their departure for Europe; some of the most intelligent surgeons of ou city have examined them and give it as their opinion that there is nothing offensive or indelicate in the exhibition, which may be attended by ladies with perfect propriety. They are about eighteen years of age, well made, of a lively disposition, very quick and intelligent, and entirely satisfied with their situation. Hours of exhibition from 9 to 1 and 3 to 6. Price of admittance 50 cents, children under 14 half price Notice is also given, that on WEDNESDAY Commencement day, and THURSDAY next, the Siam ese Youths, will be exhibited at a suitable place near the Colleges, Cambridge.   August 22

epistf

This article from the Boston Courier helped publicize the arrival of a "great natural curiosity."

Hunter and Coffin rented a giant tent, able to hold thousands of people, as the spot to exhibit Chang and Eng. The price of admission? Fifty cents—not a small price in 1829. But Robert Hunter and Abel Coffin knew they had a special feature, a show the people of Boston would pay handsomely to see. When the two promoters visited a printer to get posters made, they shared their excitement. However, when

they printed up signs advertising the twins as THE
MONSTER, Hunter and Coffin would have none of it.
The wording was quickly changed to THE SIAMESE
DOUBLE BOYS.

Once the word was out, Hunter and Coffin waited.
What if no one came to see the boys? Chang and
Eng worried about another question: What would they
do if people *did* come to see them?

Boston proved to be a city of curious spectators.
Men, women, and children flocked to the tent, eager
to view Chang and Eng. Captain Coffin or James
Hale opened the session with background informa-
tion about the twins. The authorized statements of
respected doctors were read. A member of the audience
was called to the stage to personally examine the
ligament, then testify to those gathered that this was
indeed a legitimate exhibition. Many people asked
questions. An interpreter helped the twins.

Q. Are you the same size?
A. We weigh 180 pounds. (This was their
   combined weight. Chang stood 5 feet
   2 1/2 inches tall, while Eng measured
   5 feet 3 1/2 inches. So that the boys could
   maintain a proper balance, Chang wore
   shoes with lifts.)

Q. Do you enjoy being joined together?

A. There is no choice, according to the doctors. We try to make the most of our situation.

Q. Do you mind people staring at you and asking you questions?

A. We know we are different and people are curious. It is a way of earning a living and we are grateful.

Some of the questions were more difficult, but the twins tried to answer. What if one twin believed in Buddhism but the other chose to believe in Christianity? Could both souls be saved? Or what if one twin committed a crime? Would both brothers go to jail? Was marriage possible?

Thousands of Bostonians had met Chang and Eng. Despite their good manners and charm, the twins still had most people sadly shaking their heads. One city newspaper, the *Daily Courier*, labeled the twins' joining as a "fantastical trick which dame Nature has taken it into her head to play for the special purpose of confounding the wits of us poor mortals."

By the time Chang and Eng appeared in Providence, Rhode Island, they had put together a new act. Sitting and answering questions was too dull. Now they performed somersaults and backflips. They lifted volunteers from the audience into the air and carried them around. The people cheered. Then Chang would smile. "Anyone for a game of checkers?" he'd ask. Hands would fly into the air, and someone would be picked. For the next several minutes, the crowd would be still. All attention would focus on the checkers game taking place. The twins became experts.

The people of New York City were waiting to welcome Eng and Chang when they arrived on September 18, 1829. James Hale had plastered posters and signs everywhere. The newspapers had been alerted. Each day, from nine in the morning until two in the afternoon, and then again from six until nine in the evening, people poured into the Masonic Hall on Broadway. Some of the spectators brought the two boys gifts—candy and fruit decked the front of the stage area.

Again Chang and Eng entertained their audiences with light gymnastics. Now and then someone cruelly yelled out, "Freaks!" But the two boys went on as if they had not heard. The *Evening Post* of September 21 noted that Chang and Eng "seem not only contented with their condition of forced companionship, but, so

To enliven their act, Eng and Chang performed acrobatics and played games of checkers with members of the audience.

far as we may judge from the display of their fraternal feelings during the short time that we were present with them, quite as happy as children of their age usually are."

During the three weeks the boys were in New York City, several doctors examined them. The same conclusion was reached regarding separation—it was simply too dangerous. If the fleshy band were cut, the intestines, liver, stomach, and spleen would be exposed and could become infected, concluded noted physicians Samuel Mitchell and William Anderson.

On the twins' one-week visit to Philadelphia, a doctor claimed separation *was* practicable—"though not unattended with danger," he added quickly. The same physician also admitted that he was unwilling to do the operation.

Their visit to America a financial success, Coffin, Hunter, and Hale next mapped out a trip to England. There was no need to talk Chang and Eng into the venture. They enjoyed seeing new sights and meeting new people. Occasionally they would miss their mother, but the feelings would pass quickly as they ate at a new restaurant or went for a carriage ride.

The trip to England proved uncomfortable for the twins. While their business managers enjoyed first-class cabins and treatment, Chang and Eng were assigned steerage status. For 27 days the twins ate salt beef and potatoes. They slept on a hard floor. Upstairs Coffin and Hale ate in the ship's dining hall and had private cabins with plush beds.

"It was just a mistake," Coffin said. Captain Sherburne denied that the twins were registered to receive first-class accommodations, yet he did find them better quarters. It was the first time Chang and Eng felt used and abused.

It would not be the last.

Chapter / Five

Delight and Disappointment

Inviting noted doctors to examine Eng and Chang had proven successful before the American tour. Their promoters had also worked diligently to make sure newspaper reporters received plenty of publicity about the twins. If the plan worked well in one country, why not follow it again? Since the visit to the United States had lasted only two months, there was plenty of time to repeat the procedure in the British Isles. There a 15-month tour was scheduled.

On November 24, 1829, respected members of the London medical community were invited to Egyptian Hall in Piccadilly Square. Robert Hunter, Captain Abel Coffin, and James Hale greeted each notable guest. The three hosts were all smiles as they introduced the visiting doctors to Eng and Chang. Newspaper reporters, also among the invited, hastily scribbled notes and conducted interviews. When the presentation ended, 24 doctors signed a document stating that the "remarkable and interesting" Siamese twins were everything they were advertised to be. Not only that, the physicians claimed there was nothing "offensive to delicacy in the exhibition."

The reporters were also impressed. The *Examiner* published a story noting that Chang and Eng appeared to be "cheerful and happy, and that they are in the hands of intelligent and respectable people." However, the same reporter observed that the twins "seemed to move with reluctance, and we discovered nothing of playfulness or merriment in their actions." A reporter for the *Mercury* also called attention to Chang and Eng's movements, saying that they moved across the room with "the ease and grace of a couple skillfully waltzing."

While Hunter, Coffin, and Hale carefully made plans to share the twins with the public, Chang and Eng had a chance to see London's sights. By carriage they rode to the Baker Street Bazaar with its countless vendors and markets, Covent Garden and the Haymarket theater, Surgeons' Hall, and many other attractions. Of course, the twins were attractions, too, and people gathered wherever Chang and Eng went. The two quietly answered questions, displaying the charm that had become so much a part of performances. It was clear that the two young men especially enjoyed meeting young women. The bond joining the twins might limit their movements, but it could not hold back their natural feelings.

One young woman of London society quickly fell in love with the twins. Her name was Sophia, and she shared her feelings openly, often in poetry. She sent the twins love notes and revealed her emotions to reporters. Clearly, Sophia was in love. However, when Sophia sought a legal opinion about marriage, she was told such an action could lead to a charge of bigamy, arrest, and a jail term. The thought of any such future wiped away Sophia's "undying love." She disappeared from their lives.

Chang and Eng first met the London public in December 1830. Lines formed early outside Egyptian Hall, each person willing to put out half a crown to view the visitors from Siam. For an additional charge, observers could purchase a pamphlet called *An Historical Account of the Siamese Twin Brothers from Actual Observations.*

Inside the exhibition room Eng and Chang entertained the customers. Battledore and shuttlecock was a popular British game at that time. The twins had played it in Siam. Each held a miniature racket called a battledore. The object was to hit a shuttlecock—a small cork ball with feathers on one side—back and forth. It was challenge enough for two players on a court, but with the twins only 5 1/2 inches apart, it was an amazing spectacle. The audience oohed and aahed as they watched. Chang and Eng followed a few lively games of battledore and shuttlecock with their usual acrobatics. With a light sweat coating their skin, the twins then politely answered questions from the audience. Their English was clear and grammatically correct.

Thousands of Londoners flocked to see Chang and Eng at Egyptian Hall. Chang and Eng bowed before kings and queens, princes and princesses, but by the end of the evening, the royalty was bowing to the two boys from Siam, out of genuine respect and admiration. The crowds poured in week after week. To reach more people, other theaters were rented. Visitors continued to come—over 100,000 in all.

From London, Chang and Eng headed to other English cities and towns. Audiences in Bath, Oxford, Birmingham, and Liverpool welcomed the twins warmly. Then it was off to Scotland, where an over-

AN

HISTORICAL ACCOUNT

OF THE

SIAMESE TWIN BROTHERS,
Eng and Chang Bunker

FROM

ACTUAL OBSERVATIONS.

E PLURIBUS UNUM

"UNITED WE STAND."

FOR SALE ONLY AT THE EXHIBITION ROOM.

PRICE 12½ CENTS.

THIRD EDITION—2000 EACH.

NEW-YORK:
PRINTED BY ELLIOTT AND PALMER, 20 WILLIAM-STREET.
1831.

ENG and CHANG,
THE CELEBRATED SIAMESE YOUTHS

The title page from one of the "historical accounts" of the twins that was for sale with every performance

flowing Glasgow crowd cheered the young men. The Edinburgh audience was equally friendly, and in Dublin, Ireland, people applauded for five minutes after Chang and Eng had left the stage. "They usually sleep from nine to eleven hours each night, and quite soundly," wrote one Dublin reporter. "When they feel restless and desire to change their posture, the one must roll entirely over the other, and they have been

The graceful brothers amazed London audiences with their ability to play battledore and shuttlecock, a game similar to badminton.

frequently observed to do this without either waking or being apparently disturbed by the change." Even in sleep, the twins enjoyed little privacy.

To Manchester the twins traveled, and to York and Sheffield. Each day brought a new audience, another crowd. People went away impressed with the foreign visitors.

Despite glowing reports about the twins in England, authorities in France turned down Captain Coffin's request to bring the twins there. Labeling Chang and Eng "monsters," officials feared the effect such an exhibit would have on French children. Moreover, they said, pregnant women who viewed the "monsters" might give birth to deformed children. News of the French decision troubled Chang and Eng. They had worked so hard to befriend people, yet there would always be those who would not judge them by their actions.

More disappointment followed. Robert Hunter sold his share in the twins. He wanted to return to his import-and-export business. Captain Abel Coffin also wanted a change. He headed back to the East Indies to pursue business interests, leaving his share in the twins with his wife, Susan, and a friend, Captain William Davis, Jr. James Hale remained to act as promotion agent.

Captain
Abel Coffin

By March 1831 Eng and Chang were back in America. The earlier tour had touched only four cities—Boston, Providence, New York, and Philadelphia. Now it was time to hit the smaller towns, and any other pocket of population that would pay the price to view the twins. Mrs. Susan Coffin wanted every possible penny that could be pulled from curiosity-seekers. She even bought a private buggy to carry the boys and a wagon for their luggage. Why? When they traveled by stagecoach or train, too many people got to see them for free!

Who knows how many times the twins heard themselves introduced as they crisscrossed the

United States? One night it was in an auditorium in
Ohio. The next night it was under a tent in Indiana.
Atlanta, Buffalo, Chicago—sometimes the names
were familiar. Then it was Apple Junction, Twin
Forks, Wood River. Days slipped quietly into weeks,
weeks into months. The shows continued.

Most of the people were friendly. Men shook their
hands, women gave them flowers, children simply
pointed and stared. Chang and Eng were used to the
reactions.

But then came a night in Athens, Alabama. As the
twins sat on a stage platform waiting to be introduced,
a man came rushing forward. He said he was a doctor
and demanded to examine the ligament holding the
two brothers together. Eng and Chang squirmed. It
was one thing to be inspected privately, but this was
different. Had the man not read what other doctors
had written? The twins refused the doctor's request.

"Fraud!" the man shouted to the audience. "You
are all being cheated! These are two separate men on
this stage, not one. This is a hoax—a trick!"

Eng and Chang sprang to their feet. They raced to
the doctor, pounding him with their fists. People in
the audience leaped out of their seats. Some took the
doctor's side, others sided with the twins. Stools and
chairs flew through the air, as did wild shouts and

screams. Someone emptied a pitcher of water on Chang and Eng. For several minutes the fight raged on. Finally police arrived. The doctor was released, but Chang and Eng were arrested. The twins were fined $350 for assault.

An angry Susan Coffin scolded the twins. They resented her remarks and complained to James Hale. But he had his own problems with Mrs. Coffin. Often she criticized his wife, and Mrs. Coffin claimed he was not spending enough time with Chang and Eng. In October 1831, Hale broke away from the business, bringing in a friend, Charles Harris, to help manage Chang and Eng with Mrs. Coffin. Harris, called "Doctor," would receive $50 a month for his services. That was the same amount paid Chang and Eng, in addition to their meager 25-cents-a-day allowance. Two dollars was allowed for weekly traveling fees—that is, money for horses and carriage. Captain Coffin had promised to send money regularly to their mother in Siam.

With their two-dollar-a-week expense money for horse maintenance, Chang and Eng struggled to break even. When the twins requested a dollar raise for their horses, Susan Coffin resisted. They managed to win Harris's support and received the raise. But no longer did they consider Mrs. Coffin a friend. She

*James W. Hale
in later life*

made them feel unimportant and greedy.

Neither did they feel the closeness they once had to Captain Coffin. They suspected he had been swindling them. Never were they allowed to check any financial statements, either with him or his wife. At first they had not understood such matters. But gradually they learned. They had no way of knowing how much they had earned or how much he had sent back to Siam. When they learned he had sent back only $500, the twins were outraged. They had performed for tens of thousands of people since they began. Where had all the money gone?

By June 1, 1832, Chang and Eng had reached the

age of 21. On that date they declared themselves free of any arrangement with Captain Abel Coffin. They felt they had fulfilled the agreement made in Siam over three years before and were free to pursue their own futures. To celebrate their freedom, they purchased and gave away 500 cigars.

Chapter / Six

Breaking Away

If the band of flesh that joined their bodies could not be cut, Chang and Eng hoped they could totally cut their ties with the Coffins and Captain Davis. The twins wanted to work only with Dr. Harris, whom they respected and trusted.

But a complete separation from their partners proved difficult. Letters among all the business parties reflected anger and bitterness. Captain Coffin claimed he had handled the twins fairly. Not so, Chang and Eng retorted. Both Captain Coffin and his wife had brought much unhappiness into their lives. The twins still suspected the captain of swindling them out of money.

While the arguments continued, Chang and Eng

traveled from town to town under Dr. Harris's direction. Their new business manager kept a daily record of expenses, and he welcomed their questions. Chang and Eng liked their new partner.

Dr. Harris kept Chang and Eng busy. They traveled throughout the eastern states, sometimes filling a theater or tent, at other times playing to a half-filled auditorium. The size of the audience often depended on the local economy. If times were good in an area, people came out to enjoy entertainment. If times were bad, the people stayed home.

As Eng and Chang dipped into the South, the audiences grew larger. In Tennessee and Alabama the twins pulled in $1,105 in one month, while during November and December in Mississippi they reached a total income of almost $2,500.

News of their mother back in Siam was infrequent but welcome. Late in 1833 Hunter visited Nok. Chang and Eng learned that their mother had gotten remarried, to a fisherman named Sen, and that all were in good health, including their brother and sister. "We are fully determined to go back to Siam," the twins wrote to their friend Hunter in the spring of 1834, "but cannot at present fix any time."

The longer they remained in the United States, the more Chang and Eng liked the country. Notations in

An Account of Money Received by
Chang Eng in December 1833.

			$	c
5	Vicksburg	Miss	88	25
6			65	50
7			27	50
9	Warrenton	Miss	88	"
11 12	Port Gibson	Miss	68	25
			56	"
13	Grand Gulf	Miss	46	"
14	Rodney	Miss	98	"
16	Fayette	Miss	54	"
17	Washington	Miss	58	"
18 19 20 21	Natchez	955 - 0	84	50
			87	"
			24	"
			110	"
	Carried forward $		955	"

December 1833	Brought forw.ᵈ $		955	
23	Kingston	Miss	25	
24 25	Woodville	Miss	105	
			75	
26	Fort Adams	Miss	64	
27	Pinckneyville	Miss	25	
28	St Francisville	Lᵃ	103	
30	Jackson	Lᵃ	95	
	Amount paid in Decemᵇ 1833 $		1.447	
	Deduct			
	Amount paid in dᵒ		625	2
	Balance $		821	7

The twins kept careful accounts of their finances after breaking away from Captain Coffin and his wife. This record for December 1833 shows a busy and profitable period for the brothers.

Harris's journal showed the twins buying custom-made flannel vests, buffalo robes, suspenders, black silk cravats, and suits. Grooming was important, too. They had their teeth cleaned and their hair cut often. Although Chang and Eng kept their long queues in back, their black hair was cut short in front. They bought the best sets of combs and brushes available, and new toothbrushes were purchased monthly.

During 1834 the twins spent most of their time exhibiting in the East. When incomes slipped, James Hale rejoined Harris to help manage the twins. In January of 1835, Eng and Chang sailed for Cuba. Hale had publicized the visit well; Havana was plastered with handbills and signs. The twins added a special feature to their act, puffing the Cuban cigars they both had learned to love. The people applauded wildly, causing Eng and Chang to call for some Cuban rum as well.

Hale knew that the twins liked to travel. After a few months of shows in the United States, he took them to Canada. Again the trip brought in new fans and more money.

When Dr. Harris suggested a trip to France and other European countries, the twins were surprised. Wasn't it the French officials who had called them "monsters" and forbade them to enter the country? Harris convinced the twins that times and officials had changed. Chang and Eng agreed to make the trip.

The twins arrived in Paris on December 3, 1835. Harris provided them with a servant and an interpreter. He ran big ads in the local newspapers.

Each day Chang and Eng welcomed visitors from one until four in the afternoon at the Hotel de l'Europe. The crowds were small but polite. One newspaper reporter was most impressed with the twins. He showed shame that they had once been labeled "monsters," and wrote that "the only visible part of their bodies" was the "communal part which forms as a *hyphen-mark* between the two brothers."

As usual, Eng and Chang went sightseeing every free moment. It had become a habit with them whenever they visited a new place. One reporter who followed their carriage noted that "there are times when one of the young men looks one way while his brother looks the other. For the most part, however, they look in the same direction."

Paris proved an expensive city. Harris was happy to move the twins to Belgium, then on to the Netherlands. Everywhere they went, the twins bought souvenirs, usually in the form of clothes. "Silk gloves . . . boots . . . velvet vests". . . . All were carefully noted in Harris's expense journal. "Wooden shoes" were picked up in Amsterdam, as well as three pairs of Dutch pantaloons. In June 1836 the twins headed back to the United States.

Hale and Harris quickly lined up new tours in the East and South. Once again, Chang and Eng began to travel from city to city. But more and more time was spent at Peale's Museum in New York City. Once the huge building had displayed fine art treasures

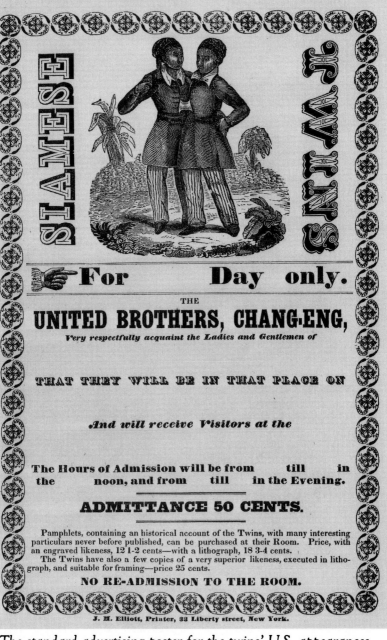

The standard advertising poster for the twins' U.S. appearances. It was printed in quantity, with the city, date of appearance, exhibition hall, and hours left blank, to be filled in when the bookings were made.

and natural history shows. But more recently Rubens Peale, the proprietor, enjoyed featuring wonders and oddities. "Clare, the Rare" was one attraction, a woman who stood a towering seven feet tall. Another audience favorite was "The Round Sisters"—Deborah Tripp, who at age three weighed 124 pounds, and her older sister, Susan Tripp, who at nearly six weighed 205 pounds. "It is a 'trip' in itself to simply walk around these two breathing balls of flesh!" declared the announcer. Chang and Eng were regular guests on the Peale's Museum stage, sometimes performing for a month at a time.

One night a visitor came backstage. Chang and Eng welcomed him into their private dressing room. He introduced himself as Dr. James Calloway of Wilkesboro, North Carolina. For over an hour the twins talked and laughed with their guest. When he invited them to vacation in Wilkesboro, they promptly accepted.

Early in 1839, Chang and Eng headed to Wilkesboro. Dr. Harris went with them, grateful for some time away from business.

Wilkesboro was a different world to Chang and Eng. They had visited the tiny town before, some two years earlier. But then it had been one of hundreds of such towns, a dot on the map where area farmers brought their families to see "The United Brothers, Chang-Eng." The twins had seen much more of the world than most 27-year-old men. But the sights of this tiny burg tucked neatly into the corner of northwestern North Carolina were unique.

Wilkesboro sat in the middle of a quilt of farmlands. Rows of cotton or tobacco graced most plots, each usually no more than 50 acres. Black slaves did the heavy work, under the careful eye of the white landowners. Most farms boasted an ample supply of cows, horses, pigs, chickens, and other livestock. Roads were poor, and a good rainstorm was apt to create a river of mud that kept people in their houses for days at a time.

Yet to Chang and Eng, there was a peacefulness to the countryside and a friendliness to the people. For ten years the twins had been on the road. They had grown weary of streets filled with carriages and buggies, of people shoving and pushing their way ahead. The staring eyes and hushed conversations as people gawked at them had become tiresome. Somehow the people of Wilkesboro seemed different. Their handshakes felt firm and friendly, their smiles and greetings seemed sincere. When they spoke, the people sounded honest and caring. They bragged about their children, of the crops harvested, and of their dreams.

And as the twins rode into the countryside, they saw mountains reaching into the sky. Clusters of trees invited picnickers, while streams snaked across rich, dark soil. This was a good place, this place called North Carolina. Chang and Eng began making plans to stay in Wilkes County. Someday, perhaps when they were rich, they would return to Siam.

The twins had managed to save over $10,000 from their exhibitions. It was not a fortune, but it was enough to rent a small store. The venture sounded exciting. That's exactly what they did. Within a few weeks of their arrival in Wilkes County, Chang and Eng stocked the shelves of a retail store. They offered everything from linens to "chawing" tobacco, from harness leather to dress patterns. Unfortunately, the times were bad for area residents. Try as they might, the twins could not turn a profit from their small store. Quickly they decided to take up farming instead. Neighbors offered to help them get started.

Despite their business problems, Chang and Eng never thought of leaving Wilkes County. After all, the people were still the same—they just did not have much money to spend. The twins built a handsome two-story home on Trap Hill. Its name had come from an old hunter who often set out a snare to catch wild turkeys.

The twins' house contained only four rooms, two downstairs and two upstairs. A giant five-foot-wide chimney serviced all four. Windows in each room stretched almost from floor to ceiling. Chang and Eng loved sunlight! The staircase leading from the ground floor to the second story was made extra wide, so that the twins could go up and down without difficulty. The kitchen, containing another huge fireplace, was built next to the house. A horse stable was also put up.

Still another nearby building was erected to house slaves and serve as a storehouse. Eng and Chang were known to work their slaves hard, offering them few luxuries in living conditions.

While their house was built with local materials, the brothers delighted in ordering furnishings from New York City. They had seen many fine items on their sightseeing ventures. Dr. Harris was dispatched to bring back rugs, candlesticks, framed pictures, silverware, and everything else needed to complete a home.

In the fall of 1839, Chang and Eng made another major decision. They knew they wanted to stay in America. But they were still citizens of Siam. In October they filed papers "to become naturalized citizens of North Carolina and the United States of America."

With their new citizenship they needed a legal surname. Other Americans had one—Smith, Jones, Johnson, Hipplethorpe. Chang and Eng remembered a family in New York City who had befriended them. In honor of these people, the twins chose the name Bunker.

By June 1840, Chang and Eng had settled into their new house on Trap Hill. They seemed to have everything they wanted and needed.

Or did they?

Chapter / Seven

The Bunker Boys Meet the Yates Girls

Chang and Eng weren't the only outsiders who enjoyed Wilkes County. Their business partner, Dr. Charles Harris, did, too. He was especially taken by the friendliness of Robert Bauguess and his family, who opened their home to the twins and Harris while the house on Trap Hill was going up.

Until now, Chang and Eng had never noticed how much fun Dr. Harris could be. Usually he was all business. But now the Irishman was often quick with a joke and a laugh, always noticing how his humor affected young Fannie Bauguess, his host's daughter.

At 38, Charles Harris spoke of finding a wife and settling down. To no one's surprise, least of all Chang's and Eng's, he announced that Fannie Bauguess was his choice. Word went out of wedding plans, which included not only the ceremony but a grand wedding supper to follow. For the people of Wilkes County, such events were cause for celebration.

The ceremony went off smoothly. Chang and Eng were part of it, positioned near the groom. Immediately following, the wedding party and guests sat down to share in the tasty treasures brought in from all parts of the county. The tables were stacked high with platters of sizzling pork and juicy venison, honey-dipped ham and pheasant. Fiddlers plucked their bows and strings, as light-stepping dancers whirled around the floor. The people of Wilkes County knew how to celebrate.

Maybe it was the sight of their good friend getting married. Perhaps romance was in the air. But when Chang and Eng caught sight of the two Yates sisters in a corner of the room, the gentlemen strolled over. Years later a neighbor who was present privately printed a book that recorded the gist of their conversation that night:

Once introduced to the sisters, Eng did not waste a moment. "My brother wants to marry," he said, "and if any young lady here will have him, we will have a wedding today."

No doubt the two Yates sisters were quite surprised, if not shocked.

Then Chang jumped in. "It is he who wants to marry and he is putting it off on me just to raise a conversation with you about love. He'd marry at the drop of a hat, and drop it himself, if he could get the ugliest girl in town to say 'yes.'"

Surely the sisters were raising their eyebrows in wonderment. But before either could speak, Eng jumped back in the conversation.

"The reason I don't marry is because I'm fast to him," he said, pointing to the ligament that held them together.

Chang repeated the same words. Then he added, "Isn't it a pity that neither of two brothers can marry because he is fast to the other?"

Finally, 18-year-old Sallie Yates spoke up. "Is there no chance for you to be separated?"

"The doctors say not," Eng answered, "and each of us decided that we would rather look on pretty girls, with a lean and hungry love-look, and continue to want a wife than to be in our graves."

This time it was 17-year-old Adelaide Yates who spoke. "What a pity that you who love ladies so dearly can't marry, and that two young ladies can't have such lovely husbands as you would have been."

Adelaide seemed to have ended the conversation. But Eng was not quite finished. "Good-bye, my brother will be back to see you some day."

"If I come back," Chang offered, "I will leave him behind because he always monopolizes the conversation of the girl I love best."

"To show that I want to be fair," said Eng, "I will let him take the choice of you girls now, and if we get back, the other shall be no less a choice to me."

The choice came easily to Chang. He pointed at Adelaide.

The foursome laughed and parted. But later, when they were alone, Chang and Eng shared their hopes. Chang thought the young women were interested, that there might be a chance. Eng was not convinced. But he smiled as he made Chang promise to take him along when he went to see Adelaide. "I will do my best to help you win her," Eng promised.

It wasn't long before the twins discovered that the Yates family home rested between their own place at Trap Hill and Wilkesboro. It was quite easy to stop by for visits on the way to and from the town.

A big surprise awaited Chang and Eng when they first met Nancy Yates, the mother of Sallie and

Adelaide. The older woman weighed 500 pounds! Yes, she understood what it was like to be a curiosity. Although she had never been exhibited, she knew well the astonished glances of strangers. Chang and Eng felt a quick friendship for Nancy Yates, feelings that the woman returned.

David Yates, with a sprawling farm of 1,200 acres worked by 15 slaves, often gave Chang and Eng advice about their ever-growing farm. Starting with 150 acres, the brothers bought any adjoining land that came up for sale. One plot was 26 1/2 acres; another measured 37 1/2 acres. The twins raised corn and hogs.

But it was clear that Chang and Eng were more interested in becoming husbands than rich farmers. They visited the Yates home more and more often in the years that followed. Finally they told the sisters they would like to marry them—Chang to Adelaide, Eng to Sallie.

Surely it was no easy decision. One can only wonder what the two young women talked about. It was one thing for Chang and Eng to be together—they had no choice. But to be married to one man with the other always there—to share meals, chores, even a bed with two men . . .

When the twins told Dr. Harris about their proposal, he was shocked. How could they even think of such a thing? They had made much of their lives so far, but this was asking too much.

Yet it did not trouble Adelaide greatly. There would be problems, to be sure, but she felt they could be worked out. She took Eng's side and agreed to talk with Sallie about his proposal. After all, it was hopeless unless all four would agree.

Slowly Sallie changed her mind. She *did* care deeply for Eng; it was the idea of spending a life with two men rather than one that bothered her.

The next matter was how to let everyone know how they felt. For the past four years, Chang and Eng had simply called on the Yates sisters at their parents' home. They had never been seen in public.

That happened one Saturday afternoon when the foursome climbed into a buggy and rode the six miles from the Yates farm into Wilkesboro. Such an act was an open admission of a romantic relationship. Eyes widened at the sight; tongues wagged. By nightfall it was the talk of the county. Assuming that David and Nancy Yates knew and approved of their daughters' conduct, an angry group marched on the Yates farm. They heaved rocks through the front windows. A bewildered David Yates appeared on the front porch of his home.

"You can't be letting your daughters take up with those Bunker boys!" someone hollered. "It ain't natural."

"God will strike you dead!" another voice shot out.

A few of the leaders talked with David Yates. It was clear he didn't know that the sisters had agreed to marry the twins; his wife didn't know, either. Returning inside, the confused man informed his two daughters that any romance with the Bunker boys was over.

Adelaide and Sallie had anticipated such a reaction from their parents. The two girls calmly tried to explain their feelings, but their parents stood firm. The Bunker boys were not welcome, and that was final!

The twins had two clergymen visit the Yates farm to try to convince David Yates that perhaps he had been too hasty. He listened but did not change his mind.

Although Chang and Eng had always been told a surgical operation for separation could kill them both, the twins made plans to have it done. Maybe that would sway the stubborn Mr. and Mrs. Yates. They even went to Philadelphia, where doctors agreed to perform the surgery. But when Adelaide and Sallie heard about it, the sisters hurried to Philadelphia, too. There would be no operation, the two young women insisted. The foursome headed back to Wilkesboro, talking about eloping.

There was no elopement. Tired and convinced that their daughters were determined to wed Chang and Eng, David and Nancy Yates gave in.

On April 13, 1843, the wedding ceremony was held in the living room of the Yates farmhouse. The guests included only close family and friends. Eng and Sallie were married first, with Chang and Adelaide taking their vows immediately afterward. Those present sat down to a delicious feast, then swirled cheerfully around the floor to the Virginia reel, a quick-stepping, knee-slapping dance everyone in the county loved.

As the party broke up, the newlyweds slipped away to Trap Hill. A special wide bed had been built to accommodate the quartet. To the wedding participants, the *Carolina Watchman* newspaper directed a humorous wish: "May the connection be as happy as it will be close!"

Chapter / Eight

Gentlemen Farmers

There were many people in Wilkes County who thought the Bunker marriages—both of them—were doomed to failure. Friendly wagers were exchanged as to just how long the brides could endure the situation. It was one thing to eat together, to wash clothes and sweep floors together, and to talk together. But what of the evening hours, the special moments when a married woman and a man share a bed together? Surely no children would come from such a union.

Surprisingly, those who thought there would be no children were wrong. On February 10, 1844, little more than nine months after their marriage, Eng

and Sallie Bunker welcomed their first child. The girl
was named Katherine Marcellus. Six days later Chang
and Adelaide greeted their first child, also a daughter,
whom they named Josephine Virginia.

It was clear that Chang and Eng were not going
to let their chest attachment limit their plans for a
family. For most of the next 20 years, either Sallie or
Adelaide as pregnant, often both of them.

In all, Eng and Sallie Bunker became parents to
11 children, 6 boys and 5 girls. After Katherine
Marcellus there were Julia Ann, Stephen Decatur,
James Montgomery, Patrick Henry, Rosalyn Etta, William Oliver, Frederick Marshall, Rosella Virginia,
Georgianna Columbia, and Robert Edmond.

Chang and Adelaide were almost as productive.
They had 3 boys and 7 girls, a total of 10 children.
Following Josephine Virginia, they welcomed Christopher Wren, Nancy Adelaide, Susan Marianna, Victoria,
Louise Emeline, Albert Lemuel, Jesse Lafayette, Margaret Elizabeth, and Hattie Irene.

Name selection for each new child posed a challenge. Family and friends received first consideration,
while Sallie and Adelaide often wanted a choice from
the Bible. They were strict Baptists and attended church
whenever possible. Chang and Eng favored names of
famous people, heroes of history.

Although they had had only minimal education, the brothers wrote with a legible hand, liked to read, and kept up with current events. They argued politics with their neighbors, favoring states' rights over federal rights. Senator Henry Clay of Kentucky was their favorite politician, and the twins declared themselves members of the Whig party. Whigs supported high tariffs on imports, and the Bunker brothers wanted the best prices they could get for their crops and livestock.

Besides keeping up with news of the day, Chang and Eng read all they could about modern farming. They fertilized the soil and bought good tools. They kept a number of slaves, up to 28 between the two of them at one time, and closely watched over their work. (One of them, Grace Gates, was given to Eng and Sallie as a wedding gift. Known as Aunt Grace, she cared for all the Bunker children and is reported to have lived to the age of 121.) The twins understood the soil, and knew that the biggest and best crops depended on how the land was treated. Harvesttime was a cause for celebration on the farmland of the Bunkers. But the celebrating was brief; Eng and Chang did not want their slaves to become "lazy." Both brothers were strict taskmasters.

With the ever-growing families, the house at Trap

Hill proved too small for everyone. There was gossip the two sisters had tired of each other and wanted to live apart. It was one thing for the twins, who had no choice, but the Yates girls had grown up on a big farm with plenty of space. Both Chang and Eng wanted their children to go to school, too, a luxury they had never had.

In 1852 the Bunkers found a house and farm for sale outside Mount Airy. The village had a school-house. It was decided Adelaide would live in Mount Airy, while Sallie would remain at Trap Hill. Chang and Adelaide's children could attend school in Mount Airy. As for Eng, he talked to James Greenwood on the next farm. Together they agreed to put up a one-room schoolhouse that their children could attend. Traveling schoolmasters who lived in with local families were common to the area. The agreement pleased all.

Chang and Eng rotated their schedules. They would spend three days at Trap Hill, then three days at Mount Airy. At the end of the third day, the twins would go to the other's home. Thoughts of ever returning to Siam to live drifted away. They kept to themselves, choosing to avoid public attention. Now and then a reporter rapped on the door, seeking a feature story. He was welcomed, fed a meal and

Aunt Grace in old age

answers, then sent on his way.

But a story that ran in the *Greensboro Patriot* on October 30, 1852, painted an ugly picture of the Bunker brothers. The article not only claimed that the men fought constantly between themselves but that they used the lash often on their slaves and horses. The twins had supposedly even split a board over the head of a man they said had insulted them!

Chang and Eng answered the article, stating that they had "endeavored to live soberly, honestly, and in peace with all the good citizens of this county." Calmly and carefully they ripped the story to shreds, detailing the flaws in each accusation. To support their own side, they included a letter signed by 13 of their friends and neighbors.

Some might have questioned the use of the term "soberly" in the twins' letter to the newspaper. It was no secret that Eng Bunker enjoyed an all-night game of poker. Although Chang did not share his brother's love of cards, he never refused a round of whiskey. His drinking sometimes led to violent arguments between the two. Angry words led to fistfights, an awkward encounter considering their positioning. Physically joined, the twins were clearly different in many ways.

Chapter / Nine

On the Road Again

Chang and Eng worked hard at being good farmers. But the money going out to pay the bills usually exceeded the money coming in from their crops. When an old friend, Dr. Edmund H. Doty, suggested that the twins exhibit themselves again, Chang and Eng pondered the thought. They had little desire to leave their homes and families. Yet if it would help the financial situation, they were willing.

In April 1849 Chang and Eng were back in New York City. Surely they remembered the days when they had first come to America, some 20 years before. The boys were in their teens then, eager to take in all the sounds and sights of a new world.

Now, however, the Bunker brothers were nearing 40. They had wives, children, property, responsibilities. Where had the years gone?

Dr. Doty booked the twins into theaters and auditoriums. If enthusiasm would bring crowds, the people would have come flocking in. But sadly enough, they did not. New Yorkers wishing to view a curiosity went to see Tom Thumb, the 25-inch-tall midget. He was a new treat to the eyes, compared with Chang and Eng, whom many had seen before. Six weeks after arriving in New York City, the group from North Carolina headed home. The trip was a dismal failure.

News of their mother's death in Siam also cast a shadow on the lives of Chang and Eng. For years they had planned to return home, yet there was always a child on the way, a crop to harvest, another expense. Now their beloved Nok was gone. They learned that their stepfather, Sen, was also dead, and they had never met the man.

The brothers thrust their energies into their farms. They kept a close watch over their slaves and worked them hard. People in the Northern states were saying that slaves were a bad thing, that no person should own another. The twins were not known to speak out politically.

In the spring of 1853, a man named Howes approached the twins about making another tour. Memories of the 1849 disaster still remained. Yet Howes insisted it would be different. Chang and Eng would be a traveling exhibit, visiting cities and towns along the eastern coastline, heading north into Canada. The twins agreed, provided they could take a child with them. Howes agreed. Eng picked Katherine, declaring it was her right, being the oldest. Chang selected Christopher.

For the next 12 months Chang and Eng were on the road. Katherine and Christopher shared the stage with their fathers, dancing to a fiddler's music and even singing a few songs. The merry group covered over 4,500 miles by boat and coach. Finally, in April of 1854, they headed home, and this time they were a bit richer for their efforts.

As the years slipped by, Eng and Sallie Bunker moved into a house in Mount Airy. Chang and Adelaide had lived in the town since 1852. The farm at Trap Hill was left in the hands of slaves to run, with the twins making daily trips by coach. With babies arriving regularly, the families kept outgrowing their homes. Eng decided to enlarge his Mount Airy house, while Chang wanted a new place. Chang found a spot about one mile from Eng's home, and the building began.

Eng and Sallie's house in Mount Airy, North Carolina

Since Chang and Adelaide had first moved out of Trap Hill, the twins shared their time equally between their homes. If the brothers were in Chang's home, Chang would be the boss. He would make the decisions and do whatever he wished. Eng remained silent, doing anything his brother wished. When the three days ended, it was Eng's turn to give the orders while Chang was the silent brother. No doubt the arrangement became strained at times, but it seemed to work.

What did *not* seem to work was their budget.

Chang and Eng labored for hours trying to figure out how to save money. But there was little one could do when a crop failed or another baby appeared. By the dawn of a new decade, the 1860s, the twins knew another tour might be useful.

The West beckoned. Chang and Eng had seen much of the country, but they had never traveled to the Far West. Even the country folks of North Carolina had heard stories about pioneers finding gold in California. It might be quite an adventure. Perhaps there would be a chance to sail to Siam, too, back to the homeland where Chang and Eng had a brother and a sister still living.

But funds would be necessary to make such a long journey. A short exhibit in New York City might earn some quick money. Chang and Eng knew the person to contact—Mr. P. T. Barnum.

Phineas T. Barnum was one of the best-known men of America. He was a super-showman, able to find exactly what people wanted to see for entertainment. Whether it was Tom Thumb, or the black nurse of George Washington, said to be 161 years old, or Jumbo the elephant, weighing over 6 tons and standing 12 feet tall, Barnum brought Americans to his exhibits. Chang and Eng were no strangers to the showman; he knew about them and only regretted

Tom Thumb and super-showman Phineas T. Barnum

that he had not discovered them himself. When they asked him to sponsor them at his American Museum on Broadway in New York City, he agreed at once. Money was money. It was what Chang and Eng and Barnum all wanted.

In October 1860 the twins opened at Barnum's American Museum. The eager crowds flocked in, some of whom had seen "the most wonderful and extraordinary human curiosities ever known" and others who had not. It was an exciting exhibit, attended by the Prince of Wales, the future king of England, Albert Edward, and other important visitors.

Proud the twins were, and richer, too, after the exhibit. However, they wanted no part of touring with a Barnum circus when it was offered. The noted showman seemed too much like the Coffins, wanting every spare penny he could make from them.

Anyway, Chang and Eng already had plans. California was calling, and the twins were eager to get started. They boarded a paddle-wheel steamer called the *Northern Light* in New York Harbor and headed south. Two of Eng's sons went along to help—and to enjoy the trip. The *Northern Light* was overcrowded. It was an eight-day journey to Panama, where the Bunker party then rode a wood-burning train that took them the short distance from the Atlantic to the Pacific

Barnum's American Museum on Broadway in New York City

side of land. Then, for 16 more days, they rode the steamer *Uncle Sam* to San Francisco.

The people of San Francisco were ready for them. A former carriage driver from New York City, Tom Maguire, was the West Coast's answer to the East Coast's Barnum. He was a first-class showman, too, but the Bunkers felt he cared about their comfort and not only the money they could make. It was a good working relationship. Maguire took out an ad in a local newspaper, the *Alta California*, announcing the twins' arrival:

The Original & World-Renowned

SIAMESE TWINS

Accompanied by Two of their Children

HAVE ARRIVED

And will Exhibit for a short time, only, at
Platts' New Music Hall,
on and after
Monday . . . December 10th, 1860.

DOORS OPEN DAILY,
(Sundays Excepted,)
from 2 to 5 P.M., and from 7 to 10 P.M.

ADMISSION 50 CENTS—
Children under 9 years of age, half price.

The newspaper also ran a feature story on the Bunker brothers that took a lighthearted approach to their appearance: "They are now fifty years of age. It is

not true that Chang is two years older than Eng, as has
been asserted—on the ground that Chang is fifty and
Eng is fifty-*too*." (Actually, the twins were only 49!)

Sadly, other stories in the *Alta California* were
not so cheerful. Election news troubled Chang and
Eng. Abraham Lincoln appeared to be winning the
presidency. The votes were still being counted. Many
leaders of the South had declared that their states
would leave the Union if Lincoln was elected. The
question of slavery was also on the minds of many
citizens. Most people in the North were against
slavery. Chang and Eng had always relied heavily on
their slaves to run their farms. What if they had to
give up their workers?

But there was nothing they could do about their
problems while they were in California. They did,
however, set aside any plans for going to Siam. Once
their tour was over, they would return to North Carolina.

Chang and Eng proved welcome guests as they
moved from city to city in California. People stood in
line to view them, and the newspaper reporters wrote
warm reviews. A Sacramento writer delighted Eng
when he wrote of the twins, "They are accompanied
by two sons—boys, of nine and twelve years old—bright
and intelligent boys."

In February 1861, Chang and Eng sailed for home. The trip had been successful, in terms of both money and crowd attendance. Yet, back home, Southern states were breaking away from the Union and forming their own Confederate States of America. War was in the air.

Chapter / Ten

War and Peace

Eng and Chang returned to Mount Airy in early March 1861. It was a different place from what they had left some four months before. Like the rest of the South, the area was bracing for war. President Abraham Lincoln, sworn into office March 4, declared that the United States would not be divided. "One Union shall prevail!" he insisted. Southern leaders continued to argue that the states had the right to withdraw from the Union if they wished.

On April 12, 1861, Confederate guns fired on Fort Sumter, South Carolina, which was federal property. A week later President Lincoln ordered a blockade of all Southern port cities. Men were called up to fight.

North Carolina withdrew from the Union on May 20 and joined the Confederate States of America.

Although Chang and Eng would not be asked to fight, both of them had sons old enough to go to war. They also learned that they would be taxed to raise money for the new Confederate army. Their wives were expected not only to maintain their own families but to sew for soldiers and nurse any wounded who might need care. As it turned out, little blood was shed in the northwest corner of North Carolina. Mount Airy and the surrounding area saw few Union soldiers.

Food prices jumped. Before the war a barrel of flour cost $18. By 1864 a barrel of flour cost $500. Bacon went from 33 cents a pound to $7.50. Many food products were impossible to get.

The Confederate treasury minted its own money and sold war bonds to raise cash. Like other Southerners, Chang and Eng bought bonds. They lent their friends and neighbors money, too. The twins felt a twinge of guilt as they watched men their own age head off to battle, leaving wives and children behind. The least Chang and Eng could do, they thought, was to help those around them deal with financial problems.

In April 1863, Chang's oldest son, Christopher,

joined the war effort by enlisting in the Confederate cavalry. The young man had just turned 18. A year later Eng's oldest son, Stephen, signed up and headed off to war.

With sons in battle, Adelaide and Sallie became increasingly tense. They feared hearing the news that so many of their friends had received—that a son had been lost or killed.

Sharing their wives' concern about their sons, Chang and Eng also worried about financial matters. At first most Southerners believed the war against the North would be quick, lasting a few weeks, possibly a month or two. But as the months became years and the cost of lives and war machinery increased, the value of Confederate money decreased. Loans to neighbors remained unpaid.

In August 1864, Christopher Bunker was wounded and captured by Union soldiers. The news stunned the Bunker families. A month later the families learned that Stephen Bunker had also been wounded in battle. The mood darkened further in the homes of both Chang and Eng.

Throughout the four long years of the Civil War, the people of the United States lived in fear. In the South it was not only the presence of Union soldiers that caused concern. Many Southerners sided with the

Northern cause. It was difficult to know who was the enemy.

Although Chang and Eng Bunker clearly stood on the Southern side, they were not vocal about their politics. When the Civil War finally ended in April 1865, the Bunker families sighed with relief. Both Christopher and Stephen returned to Mount Airy, bringing the first joy their families had known for a long time.

Serious problems remained, though, for former slave owners and for former slaves. After the Union had defeated the Confederacy, the slaves were set free. Chang had owned 12, valued at $9,500, while Eng had owned 21, worth over $17,000. The 33 slaves left the farm, but many returned when they could not find work elsewhere. Now, of course, they received wages, like other workers. The Confederate money the Bunkers had, however, was worthless, and the money they had lent did not come back. Too many of the families who had borrowed the money had lost loved ones and land. They could not repay their debts.

Desperate, Chang and Eng took to touring again, mostly in the Midwest. They had a new manager named Judge H. P. Ingalls. At 54, the twins could no longer perform acrobatics, but spectators seemed satisfied at just listening to the men talk about their lives. The fact that Eng had fathered 11 children and Chang 10 amazed their audiences. Now and then someone would question how this was physically achieved. The twins would only smile and ask for another question.

In 1866, Chang and Eng returned to New York City. This time they appeared at Union Hall, sharing the stage with Hoomio and Iola, the "wild Australian children." The unusual boy and girl displayed fang-like teeth and pointed ears and heads; they could scream like angry jungle birds. One newspaper reporter noted the contrast between the acts, stating, "The friendly, gentle voices of the famed Siamese twins is a welcome change from the screeching of the strange young creatures from 'down under.'"

In August 1867, Chang's daughter Josephine Virginia Bunker suffered a heart attack and died. Only 23, the young woman had accompanied her father and uncle on many of their tours. She had also cared for a sister and brother, Louise and Jesse, both of whom were deaf-mutes. Josephine's loss was keenly felt in Chang and Adelaide's home.

A month later Eng and Chang were touring once more. Judge Ingalls had arranged a trip for them to New York City to meet with P. T. Barnum again.

It was a hopeful reunion in many ways. Barnum's

Eng with his 15-year-old son, Patrick Henry, and Chang with his arm around his 8-year-old son, Albert. In their fifties, the twins were forced to go back on the road to make up the money they'd lost during the Civil War.

New American Museum had burned down the previous March, and he was struggling to make a comeback. Still a clever showman, he planned a double feature of creatures: he would send Tom Thumb and his new midget wife around the world, and Chang and Eng would tour England.

The twins accepted the offer. They were 57 now, with most of their lives behind them. They had married and fathered children. They had met hundreds of thousands of people, the rich and the poor, the famous and the unknown. They had seen Paris and London and New York City and so many other cities and towns. Yet one wish lingered. They longed to be individuals, separate beings who could walk and sit and lie alone. Adelaide and Sallie wanted it, and so did their children. Without knowing it, P. T. Barnum offered them a final chance to make their wish come true. No doctor in the United States would operate on them. Perhaps, just perhaps, there might be someone in England who would. It was worth a try.

Chapter / Eleven

Last Chances

P. T. Barnum knew how to get the public's attention, whether it was the American public or the British public. Although Eng and Chang did not tell the showman about their plans to pursue a surgical separation, Barnum concocted his own story about the twins' seeking a separation. It was, Barnum reasoned, a way to get extra publicity, and the showman spread the news.

But the American promoter did not know that another Bunker hoped to talk to some foreign doctors, too. Kate, 24, Eng's oldest daughter, was suffering from an unknown illness. She grew steadily weaker. Perhaps one of the overseas specialists might be able

LAST APPEARANCE
Of the Original and World-Renowned
SIAMESE

T W I N S !

CHANG & ENG
AND THEIR CHILDREN.

☞ These Wonderful Living Curiosities

Who have so long excited the wonder and astonishment of the world
are now on their way to Paris to subject themselves to the critical and
perhaps fatal operation of surgical separation.—This they have long
held in contemplation, and now having reached the rapid decline of life
and fully conscious that by the unchangeable laws of nature, but a very
brief period at most is allotted them on Earth, have finally decided to
submit to the trying ordeal, whatever the result.   Now on Exhibition
for a short time only at

616 BROADWAY,
(Near Houston,) prior to their departure.

HOURS OF EXHIBITION
From 9 to 12 A. M.; 2 to 5 P. M.; 7 to 10 P. M.

ADMISSION........................35 CENTS
Children under 10................25 Cents

Clarry & Reilley, Printers and Engravers, 12, 14 & 16 Spruce St.

to help. Anyway, the cruise itself might bring back her strength. Twenty-one-year-old Nannie Bunker, Chang's oldest living daughter, went along, too. Barnum wanted the British audiences to view not only the Siamese twins but their totally normal, beautiful daughters.

Nannie kept a diary of the trip. She was seasick most of the two-week journey, and so were many of the passengers. But Chang and Eng, seated at a chess-board and puffing on cigars, seemed to be in the best of health.

England greeted the Bunkers with cold and fog. They headed to Scotland to talk with the famed doctors at the Edinburgh Medical College. Chang and Eng insisted Katherine be examined first. The doctors complied, then shared the results. It was not good news. Katherine was suffering from "pneumonary consumption," which was incurable. Some relief of pain was possible, but the end was in sight.

Next it was Chang's and Eng's turn. How many times had they been examined by doctors in their lives? Hundreds, perhaps thousands. Maybe, just maybe, this time would be different.

Eager to learn the results, Chang and Eng had to wait. The Christmas holidays caused some delay, and then there were additional tests. Their exhibits gave them a chance to forget about the surgical possibilities.

This poster advertising the twins' last public appearance, in New York City, includes the story that the brothers were determined to undergo surgical separation.

However, Nannie found the public appearances frightening. It was her first time before an audience. Yet newspaper reporters wrote of Nannie's and Kate's grace and charm, praising their families back home for having raised such fine young women. The remarks boosted Kate's spirits and offered Nannie confidence.

But there was little that would boost the twins' spirit and confidence when they learned the results of their examinations. Sir James Simpson concluded that the operation was possible, but that it would be "so perilous in its character that the twins could not, in my opinion, be justified in submitting to it, nor any surgeon justified in performing it." Strangely enough, Dr. Simpson also felt it was not Chang's and Eng's desire to be separated but rather that of "some of their relatives." The twins were shocked. Certainly Sallie and Adelaide had voiced that wish often enough, but Chang and Eng truly wanted it themselves. But the decision was clear—there would be no operation.

A visit to Queen Victoria at Buckingham Palace in London proved a brighter moment. The monarch presented each brother with a gold watch and chain personally engraved. The jewelry became an instant family treasure.

Eager to get Kate home safely, the Bunkers sailed for New York City on July 30, 1869. Sixteen days later they were back in Mount Airy. Nannie opened a trunk to reveal over 100 gifts she had bought for the relatives. Rolls of silk and calico, skirt hoops, plaid vests, rings and bracelets, books, gloves—each present she pulled out met a loud round of squeals and applause.

Judge Ingalls set up a fall tour for Chang and Eng into the West and Northwest. The twins performed at farm fairs, sharing some of their own experiences of raising crops in North Carolina.

But when a British entertainment manager named Wallace contacted them about returning over-seas, Chang and Eng showed interest. They had met Wallace on their last trip to England, and they liked him. He suggested they tour France, Germany, Russia, Spain, and Italy. By this time, the Bunker children all begged to go along. Chang chose his 12-year-old son, Albert, while Eng picked 21-year-old James. The boys promised to follow Nannie's example and bring back presents for everyone.

In February 1870 the four Bunkers and Wallace boarded the steamer *Allemagne*. Once across the Atlan-tic, they headed to Germany. The Circus Renz in Berlin featured elephants, lions, and a high wire act. Chang and Eng had never performed in a circus before. They appeared stiff and stern, clearly not comfortable with all the blaring music. The crowds laughed at them, making the twins even more miserable.

These painful experiences made Chang and Eng more eager to find a physician who might cut them apart. One noted surgeon, Dr. Berend of Berlin, asked to examine them, with the help of three other doctors. Their verdict—no operation. Such surgery "could possibly cause the opening of the abdomen and endanger their lives," the team concluded.

A final hope remained. Dr. Rudolf Virchow was considered among the best surgeons in the world. The first physician to describe leukemia, he was the director of the Pathological Institute in Berlin. Chang and Eng requested an examination, and Dr. Virchow agreed.

For more than an hour the doctor inspected the twins. Chang and Eng could not hide their discomfort, especially when Dr. Virchow pricked their adjoining cord with a needle. Over the years, the two men had endured many inspections of this kind. But this time, they hoped, the examination might bring good news.

It was not to be. Dr. Virchow recommended against separation. Although convinced that the twins had organs independent of the other, Dr. Virchow thought that the cord between them might hold important blood vessels. Massive bleeding could occur if severed. No, there was too big a risk.

The news was a bitter blow to Chang and Eng.

Dr. Rudolf Virchow, the last physician Eng and Chang consulted about being separated

Disappointed and discouraged, they promised to accept their condition. What years they had left, they would live together as they always had.

Russia offered a brief uplift to the tour. Czar Alexander II treated the Bunkers like special visitors. They were welcomed into the palace, where they attended a play in the royal box. Twelve-year-old Albert, Chang's son, was caught holding the hand of one of the czar's daughters.

But the rest of the European tour came to a sudden and quick end. On July 19, 1870, France declared war on Germany. Americans were advised to head home. The Bunker family and Wallace boarded a steamer in Germany and set sail for New York City.

Chang and Eng were reported to be quieter than usual on the trip home. They spent most of the time playing chess. It was on the seventh day at sea that Chang suffered a stroke. After that, things were never the same.

Eng and Chang in later years

Chapter / Twelve

A Quiet Exit

Although Chang gradually regained some strength, the years from 1870 until 1873 were quiet ones for the Siamese twins. Chang's oldest son, Christopher, took over running the family's farm and 350 wooded acres. Chang was said to be worth some $23,000, a handsome amount in those days.

Eng's farm was smaller, 100 acres. His cash value was said to be approximately $7,000.

Early in January 1874, attention focused on the homes of Chang and Eng Bunker. Most folks in the area knew the schedules of the brothers. For 22 years they had rotated between their wives and families three days at one house, then three days at the other.

The pattern never changed. Even when Dr. William Hollingsworth told people he had been out to Chang Bunker's place on January 13, people knew the brothers would be headed to Eng's home on the 15th. Only death could change the long-established routine.

Ever since Chang's arrival at Eng's home the night of Thursday, January 15, he had been irritable and restless. On Friday he had trouble breathing. The brothers made frequent trips to the front porch to take in some of the cold, fresh air. But that night Chang could not sleep. Eng slept soundly. In the early morning hours, Chang woke Eng. They added logs to the fire and sat watching the flames lick at the wood. Finally Eng persuaded Chang to go back to bed.

About four in the morning, Eng's son William looked in on the two men. He was pleased to find his father snoring. Yet when the boy rounded the bed and turned up the kerosene lamp to see his uncle, William gasped. The boy touched his uncle's cheek as Eng awakened.

"William, I feel mighty sick," his father said. "How is your Uncle Chang?"

"Uncle Chang is cold," the boy answered. "Uncle Chang is dead."

Alarmed, Eng studied his brother closely. "Then I am going!" he said.

William turned and raced from the room. In moments, everyone in the house was awake. Sallie sent for Dr. Hollingsworth. There might still be time to save her husband, she thought. Then she took her place at Eng's bedside, rubbing his arms and legs as he requested. "I am very bad off," he whispered, a cold sweat covering his body. His children took turns rubbing his body, pulling and stretching his limbs as he ordered. The minutes ticked away.

Eng gazed at his brother. Sixty-three years they had been together. Now he pulled his brother to him in a final embrace. Looking around at his family, Eng whispered, "May the Lord have mercy on my soul." His eyes closed and he slipped into a deep sleep.

Shortly after six o'clock the Hollingsworth carriage rolled up to the Bunker front gate. The doctor grabbed his bag of surgical instruments and raced into the house.

But it was too late. Just as Eng had lived his life with his brother Chang, he had died with him, too. It was January 17, 1874.

Adelaide was summoned and expressed disappointment she had not been sent for earlier, when the doctor had been. But grief swiftly swept away her displeasure. Later that day the women prepared their husbands for public viewing. Friends and neighbors

Robert Bunker, Eng's youngest child. He was the last of the twins'
children, dying at age 85 in 1951. Here he is photographed in
Eng's Mount Airy house beside the bed in which the twins died.

would want to pay their respects.

Dr. Hollingsworth and others voiced new concerns. What about a postmortem to determine the cause of death for both men? No, the widows wanted none of that. What of vandals, then? The bodies of Chang and Eng would never be safe from grave robbers. The corpses could be stolen and exhibited.

The two wives were horrified at the thought. They were equally shocked at the suggestion that they might sell the bodies for profit.

On Sunday the people of Mount Airy and surrounding areas called to pay their respects. Chang and Eng were dressed in black suits, the handsome attire they had toured in. But there would be no funeral or services until all the children returned home.

That day came and went quietly. Only the families gathered to bid Chang and Eng farewell. The bodies, laid in a walnut casket surrounded by a tin casing, were buried in the basement of Eng's home. It was cool there, and the bodies would be preserved until it was safe to bury the twins in a permanent spot elsewhere.

But Adelaide and Sallie soon faced another decision. Dr. William Pancoast of Philadelphia, representing many other noted physicians, asked if they might examine Chang and Eng. Finally, secrets of the connecting ligament could be explored, secrets that had mystified doctors for almost 50 years.

The widows agreed. First Dr. Pancoast arrived to examine the bodies in Mount Airy. It was quickly determined that the Eng home was not suitable for a complete examination. The bodies were embalmed and shipped to the Mütter Museum of the College of Physicians in Philadelphia.

On February 18, 1874, the findings were announced. In brief, the doctors discovered that the livers of both men "push through the respective peritoneal openings into the band." In other words, the flesh that joined Chang and Eng contained important liver tissue. The twins could have died in any operation. The doctors also concluded that Chang had died of a cerebral blood clot, while Eng had died of shock and fright.

The doctors at the Mütter Museum asked to keep the joined livers of the twins. The organs could be preserved in formalin. But when the bodies of Chang and Eng were returned to Mount Airy, it was discovered that the lungs and intestines were missing. Once more the Siamese twins posed another mystery— even after their deaths. Members of the Bunker family demanded explanations, but received few answers.

For a year the bodies of Chang and Eng Bunker lay buried in Eng's cool cellar. A layer of charcoal covered the coffin. It was not until the spring of 1875 that the bodies were reburied on the lawn of Chang's home. In 1917, following Adelaide's death, the twins' coffin was unearthed and reburied next to Chang's wife. The grave presently sits behind a Baptist church

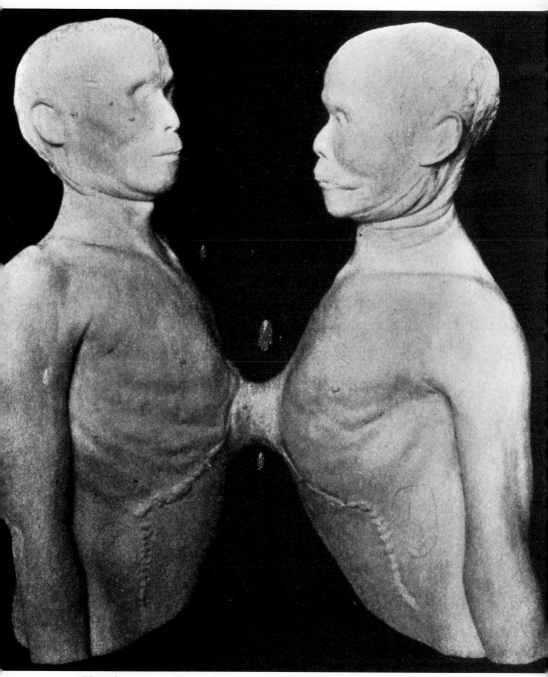

The plaster cast that doctors made of Eng and Chang after the autopsy

The double gravestone of Eng and Chang

in White Plains, North Carolina. Although the double headstone indicates that Sallie is buried there also, her remains lie on Eng's farm. Thousands of sightseers visit the cemetery each year. Many wonder aloud, "How many brothers could claim the same birth date and death date?"

And then there are the children of the area who grow up asking, "When does one plus one equal one?" Boys and girls delight at the puzzled expressions they evoke. "When you are Eng or Chang Bunker!" comes the squealed answer, with no disrespect intended. And it is likely that the listener knows the story of the amazing Siamese twins, those two men who lived and died like one. As P. T. Barnum used to say about the Bunker brothers, "They're the real thing, ladies and gentlemen, incredible but true!"

It was one time the super-showman did not exaggerate.

Milestones in the Life of Eng and Chang Bunker

1811 Eng and Chang are born in Meklong, Siam, on May 11.

1825 Eng and Chang visit King Rama III of Siam in Bangkok.

1827 Eng and Chang visit Cochin China as representatives of Siam.

1829 Eng and Chang sail to the United States.

Eng and Chang go on public exhibit for the first time.

1839 Eng and Chang become naturalized United States citizens.

Eng and Chang purchase home landsites in Wilkes County, North Carolina.

1840 Eng and Chang move into their farm home known as Trap Hill.

Eng and Chang select the surname Bunker in honor of a New York City family who had befriended them after the brothers came to America.

1843 Chang Bunker marries Adelaide Yates on April 13.

Eng Bunker marries Sarah (Sallie) Yates on April 13.

1860 Eng and Chang are exhibited for the first time by Phineas T. Barnum.

1869 Eng and Chang are presented to Queen Victoria of England.

1874 Eng and Chang die on January 17.

For Further Reading

Bowring, John. *The Kingdom and People of Siam.* (Volumes 1 and 2) London: Oxford University Press, 1969.

Clair, Colin. *Human Curiosities.* London: Abelard-Schuman, 1968.

Clemens, Samuel L. *Pudd'nhead Wilson and Those Extraordinary Twins.* Baltimore: Penguin Books, 1960.

Drimmer, Frederick. *Very Special People.* New York: Amjon Publishers, 1973.

Edwards, Frank. *Strange People.* New York: Lyle Stuart, 1961.

Hunter, Kay. *Duet for a Lifetime.* New York: Coward-McCann, 1964.

Sutton, Felix. *Master of Ballyhoo: The Story of P. T. Barnum.* New York: Putnam, 1968.

Wallace, Amy, and Irving Wallace. *The Two.* New York: Simon & Schuster, 1978.

Wells, Helen. *Barnum, Showman of America.* New York: David McKay, 1957.

/Index